PAPER BOATS

Fold & Float Your Own Origami Boats

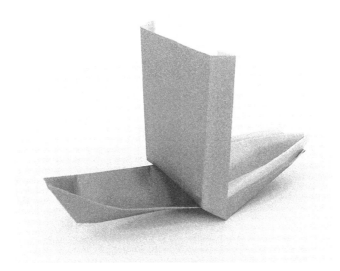

Carmel D. Morris

Walk Da Plank Publications

Copyright: Carmel Morris
First published by Harper Collins 1990 as *Fold Your Own Boats*
Reprinted 1991, 1992, 1993, 2011, 2020, 2023, English, Español, Deutsch,
Français, Italiano, Nederlands, Português editions.
This edition published by Walk Da Plank, an imprint of Gryphon Chess, 2023
ISBN: 978-0-6458839-0-9
Cover design and photography: C Duryea
Typeset in Palatino Linotype 11pt
10 9 8 7 6 5 4 3 2 1
The right of Carmel D. Morris to be identified as the author has been asserted
in accordance with the Copyright, Designs and Patents Act, 1988
Apart from any fair dealing for the purpose of review, private study, research
or criticism, as permitted under the Copyright Act, no part may be
reproduced by any process, including digital and apps, without written
permission.

Preface

Aircraft Carrier

Welcome to a whole new world of paper folding for the high seas. If you like origami but find it difficult to make the more complicated models, this book covers all bases; from simple to moderately complex. Although most models are easy to fold, many are fold-only. To make it easier for the young ones, the author is happy to use the occasional scissor snip to get the job done. So there is a model and skill level for everyone in the family.

So grab a sheet of colored paper, wax paper or waterproof chocolate wrapper and start folding. You'll amaze your friends with your newfound shipwright skills.

Happy folding and bon voyage!

Important note when folding

Various paper sizes are used in this book. Models are designed for all the family, therefore a few models will have some cut and tape steps; others may use two pieces of paper while more complex models will only use one sheet of paper with no cuts.

It is very important to practice all the basic steps before starting on the models themselves. Before commencing, try the reverse folds, rabbit ear fold, plus the other fold exercises several times before starting.

By following the symbols, folding guides and instructions in this book, your boats are sure to be more realistic when finished and will float when correctly folded.

Contents

Preface 3

Introduction 6

Folding Techniques 10

Canoe 12

Gondola 16

Row Boat 21

Speedboat 28

Sailing Boat 33

Two-in-one Yacht 41

Easy Catamaran 50

Rich Dude Cruiser 58

Seaplane 64

Pirate Ship 71

Ocean Liner 79

Aircraft Carrier 85

Introduction

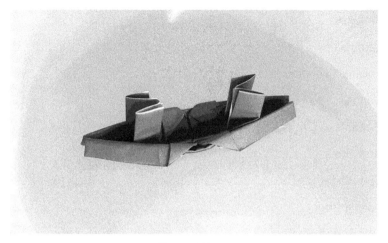

Ocean Liner

Ahoy me little sea captains! For thousands of years people have crossed the waters of the globe in craft of all shapes and sizes, kayaks and canoes, galleys and galleons, sailing ships and steamers, fishing boats and rowing boats, plus luxurious passenger craft.

Stories of romance and adventure on the high seas abound. There are tales of the Vikings who traded and plundered, of the Spaniards who sailed the galleons in search of treasure and lands to conquer; of intrepid explorers in search of new worlds, and villainous pirates who struck fear into the heart of many a sailor.

If you are an aspiring seafarer, if you love the feel of the wind in your hair and salt spray on your face, or if you just love mucking about in boats, then welcome to the fun world of paper watercraft.

With the models shown in this book, you'll be able to create your own nautical adventures on boating ponds, local streams, rivers, rapids, the beach, or even the high seas… in your bathtub.

Some models are easy to make, even the clumsiest deckhands will be whittling their own paper watercraft to perfection and will 'learn the ropes' in no time.

You're encouraged to invent your own craft too since anything is possible with paper, or plastic sheeting for more permanent water use.

The Shipwright Stuff

Believe it or not, this book will elucidate you to some pretty nifty geometry as used in shipbuilding. Once you have mastered the paper boats, you may like to try your hand at cardboard or wooden craft. The shapes are the same, only the material differs.

It's quite possible to make a life-sized version of a boat in this book. People have done it already (I recall as a child reading about a man who made a full-sized Origami rowboat out of newspaper that actually floated (after some considerable waterproofing using acrylic paint)).

Inches and millimeters are used in various places throughout this book, so have a ruler handy that has both metric and imperial measurements.

Finally, read the instructions carefully and practice the folds shown at the front of this book before you start. Once you have mastered the basic steps, you won't be left high and dry.

Types of material to use

Models in this book are made from square paper or Letter/A4 with some trimming to get the right proportions, but the size is up to you. Some models use off-cuts from paper used for other boats. It's an efficient way to make useful boats.

I suggest you also try larger sheets of paper such as A3 or sheet card. Multi-colored waterproof wrapping paper would be ideal for boats on long voyages.

Paper must be crisp, not too heavy and be able to retain a fold without 'falling open'.

For waterproofing paper, try lacquer spray on your model when it is completed.

Aircraft carriers are more suited to a metallic look and aluminum foil is ideal. However, aluminum cooking wrap is too thin so you would need to reinforce it with paper underneath.

Use spray adhesive to stick a sheet of aluminum foil to a sheet of paper; that way the boat will be easy to fold.

Acetate, that is, plastic sheets as used in some inkjet and laser printers is ideal for making a boat that you wish to keep.

Provided the plastic is not too thick, it should be easy to fold.

Note that when folding, some plastics retain the fold, especially if well creased. This is known as 'plastic memory'; therefore make sure your folds are correct the first time round, otherwise you will have to start again with a new sheet of plastic.

Remember to respect the environment, it is suggested to first only practice with old paper found around the house, such as junk mail.

When you've finished with your model, don't throw it out. Give it to a friend, or make a paper boat mobile for the younger ones (if you have any in your family) or play racing games in the swimming pool, bathtub etc.

Folding Techniques

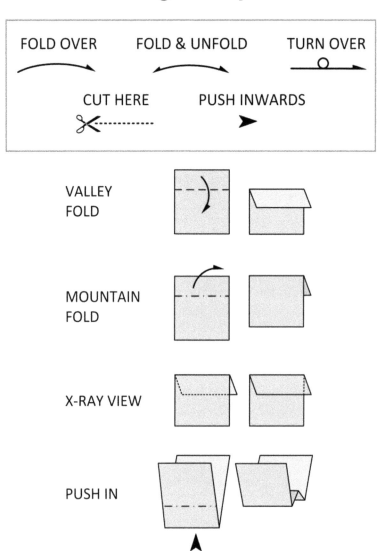

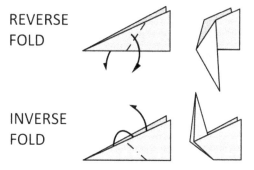

REVERSE FOLD

INVERSE FOLD

Rabbit Ear Fold

Make a diagonal crease-fold, and then two intersecting crease-folds that meet the first diagonal. Bring in the sides and pinch together to form a point, and then flatten it.

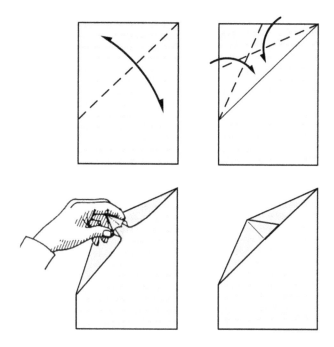

Canoe

Now you can have your very own 'dugout'. If you make a huge version it could look like a tanker, especially if you fold a few boxes to place inside to look like cargo.

Canoe step 1

Using Letter or A4 paper, fold lengthwise in half.

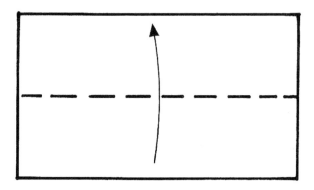

Canoe step 2

Fold the corners by an inch or three centimeters.

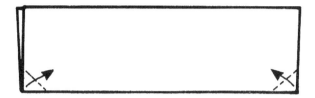

Canoe step 3

Fold the top flap down so that it partially covers the folded corners.

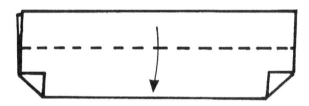

Canoe step 4

It should look like this. Turn the paper over.

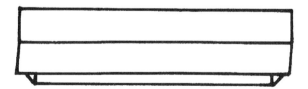

Canoe step 5

    Fold the side in to lock the corner folds.

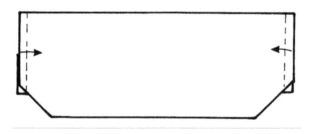

Canoe step 6

    Fold opposite top flap down.

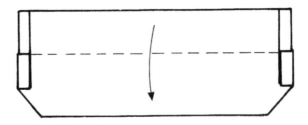

Canoe step 7

    Crease-well the hull area, and then hold sides at the center and pull to open out the canoe.

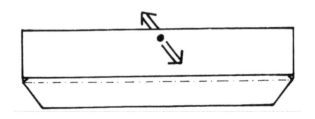

Canoe step 8

Almost there, with model upside down, push in the ends where they jut out. Squash and flatten the fold to the underside and then turn the boat back over.

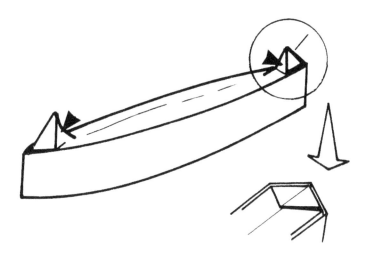

Your canoe is complete. If you're at a pool party, float one of these to a friend. Make sure you fill it with candy first!

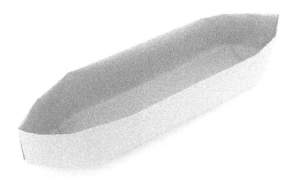

Gondola

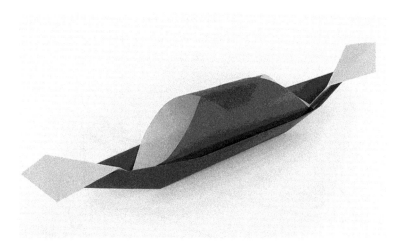

If you live in Venice, you may be catching one of these (also known as a *traghetti*) to school or the office.

This model has the traditional 'felze', or center cabin. Although not quite a flat bottomed boat, you could with some push-in techniques create your own flat bottom so try experimenting.

Gondola step 1

Use a square of black paper (traditionally, Gondolas are painted black). The paper I used was black on one side and white on the other. If you have paper like this, first have the paper positioned white side up.

Crease-fold the paper diagonally in half, unfold, then fold point 'A' down in approximate location shown, and then fold flap upwards along the center crease as shown in lower left image. Repeat for the opposite side.

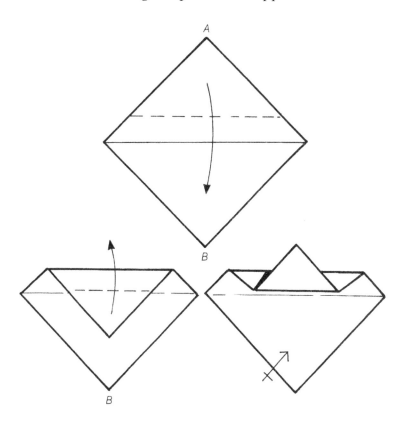

Gondola step 2

Fold behind the corners to lock the triangle sections.

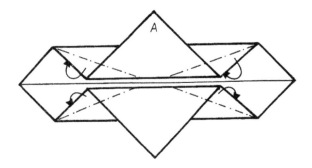

Gondola step 3

Fold in half.

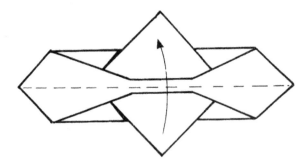

Gondola step 4

Crease-well and push the ends inside out.

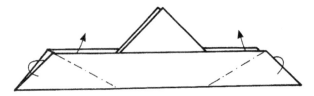

Gondola step 5

Crease the triangle sections on each end and flatten out while holding at each end the areas marked 'X'.

Now curve the center triangles to make the cabin.

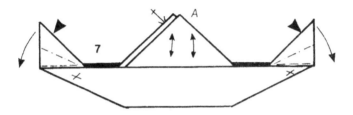

Gondola step 6

Cabin section shown; either cut a slit into one triangle section and slot the point of the other into it, folding back underneath, or simply use tape to hold the two sections together to make the cabin.

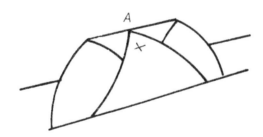

Your completed Gondola; you may need to add some center weight for ballast should it tip to one side. A coin would work.

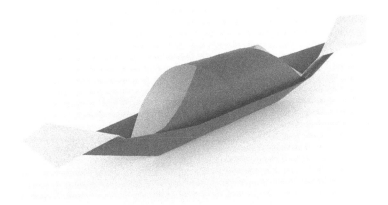

Alternatively, experiment by folding a quarter inch up from the bottom of the boat and pushing inwards and then flattening the bottom.

This technique is shown in other models in this book.

Row Boat

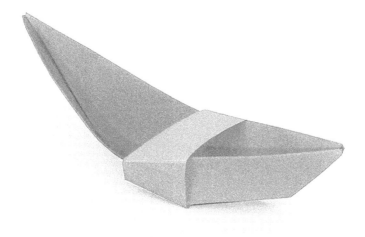

A simple craft with a seat; row boats go all the way back to galleys in ancient times where many rowers would be busy keeping their much larger craft moving.

Row boats were more maneuverable than sailing craft and many ancient designs persisted over the centuries.

Row Boat step 1

Cut a Letter or A4 sheet lengthwise in half and using one half, fold the right end across in the approximate position shown (less for a smaller seat, more for a larger seat).

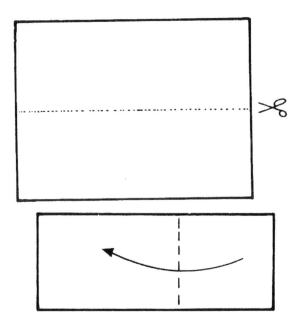

Row Boat step 2

Fold in half.

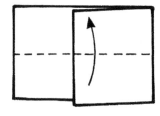

Row Boat step 3

Fold top edge down and leave about a quarter inch (7mm) showing below, and repeat for the other side.

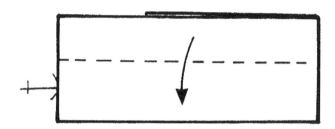

Row Boat step 4

Make a diagonal crease-fold at 45 degrees on both sides. We will use the upper flap to make the seat.

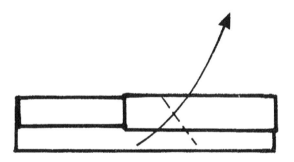

Row Boat step 5

Unfold the diagonal and open the model out. Noting the creases, lift up the upper flap. Push in where shown on the lower image and then collapse the fold.

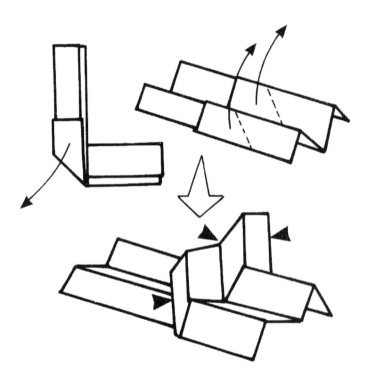

Row Boat step 6

Fold back the outer corner flaps on each end, and then tuck bow and stern corner diagonals behind them.

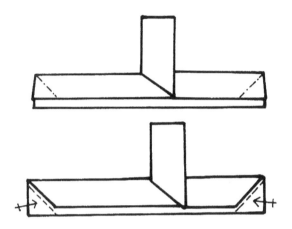

Row Boat step 7

Fold behind outer bow (left) flaps at new angle, and tuck in to lock the bow section.

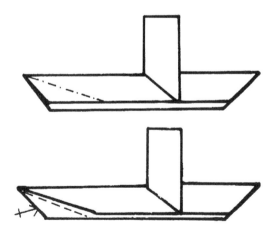

Row Boat step 8

Gently pull the sides apart to open pen out the model and then swing down the 'sail' section to make the seat.

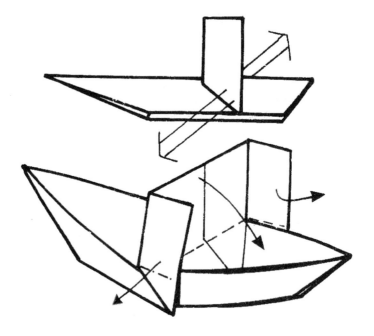

Row Boat step 9

Looking down on your craft, fold the sides down and flatten against the hull. In the lower image; tuck the jutting corners on both sides in to secure the seat.

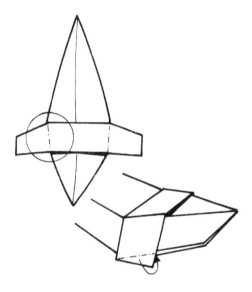

Your finished rowboat; this craft will float well and is very stable. To make them last longer, spray with clear vinyl paint all over.

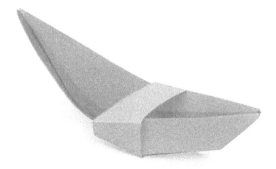

Speedboat

I was told by friends that this looks a bit like a Spencer runabout.

This craft obviously won't be able to go as fast but if you're at a pool party, make your boat in plastic wrapping, add some string to the bow and it should be able to take some pressure as you pull it across the pool.

Try having a race with your friends in choppy waters!

Speedboat step 1

The folding procedure is similar to the Rowboat.

Use a sheet of Letter or A4 cut lengthwise in half. Fold one end in half (right-hand image) and then fold the bottom edge of the upper flap up by about one-sixth (lower left image).

Once you have done this, fold the model lengthwise in half (bottom right image).

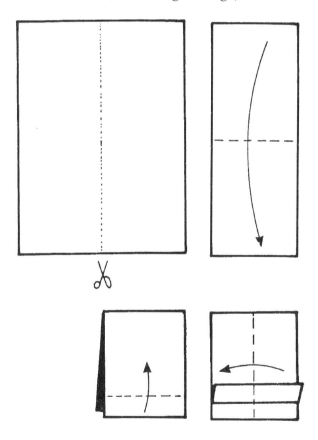

Speedboat step 2

Position the model facing you horizontally. Fold both sides down and then (lower image), grip where circled and pull up the center section by about 30 degrees. This will be our 'windshield'.

Lifting the section may be a bit tricky, so patience is required; the entire flap must be angled upwards so you would need to open out the boat a bit to raise the center fold.

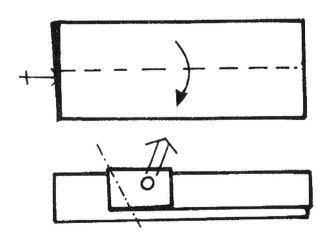

Speedboat step 3

Fold end corners in as for rowboat to make bow and stern, and then (middle image) fold the center flaps behind to hold the windshield.

The lowermost image is an enlarged view; tuck the flaps in to lock the windshield and then gently pull out the boat sides to reveal the 'windshield'.

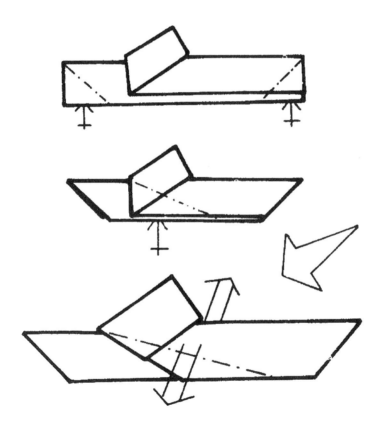

Speedboat step 4

Fold back the upper edge of the windshield and then (lower image) crease where indicated to reinforce the windshield if necessary.

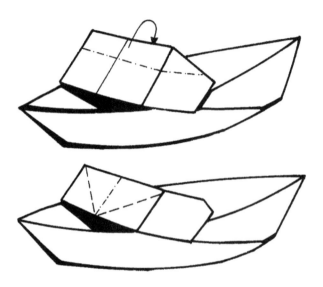

Your finished speedboat is ready to race in the swimming pool, bathtub, storm water drain, creek, etc.

Sailing Boat

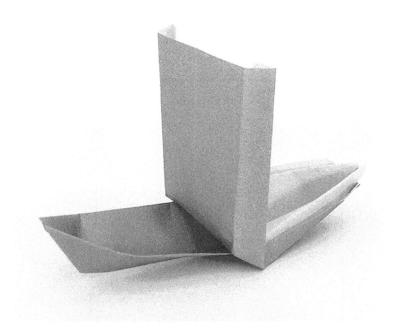

This is more like a sailing skiff, a kind of dinghy with a sail.

Place in the swimming pool or bathtub and blow the paper sail to make it move fast.

When waterproofed with spray vinyl or lacquer, your boat will last longer.

Sailing Boat step 1

Similar to the row boat, this model uses one half of Letter or A4 paper cut in two (you can make two boats!).
Lower diagram: fold in half.

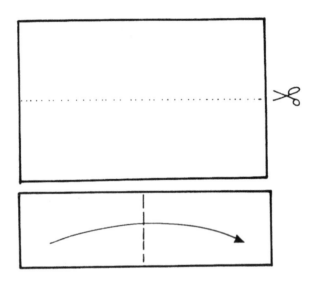

Sailing Boat step 2

Larger view; fold the edges of the upper flap towards each other, pushing in the left corners and flattening the fold.

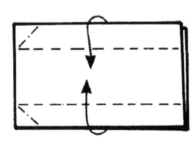

Sailing Boat step 3

Fold in half.

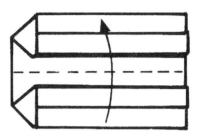

Sailing Boat step 4

This image shows an enlarged view.

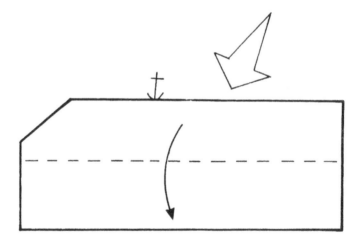

Fold top edge down and repeat on other side.

Sailing Boat step 5

Crease-fold the right-hand side at a 45 degree angle; crease on both sides but fold upwards only the upper sail section flap.

You'll see in the lower image the side edges of the sail flip around. Make sure you follow the crease position but fold against the crease in the opposite direction.

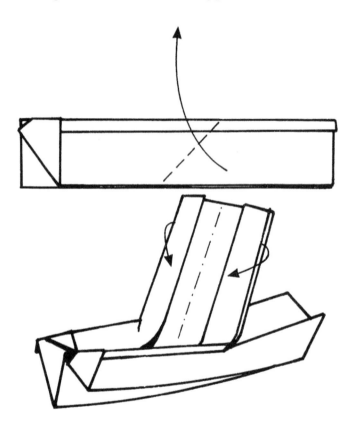

Sailing Boat step 5 (cont.)

Almost there…; the outer sail edges fold backwards and the center sail section is made flat to complete the sail.

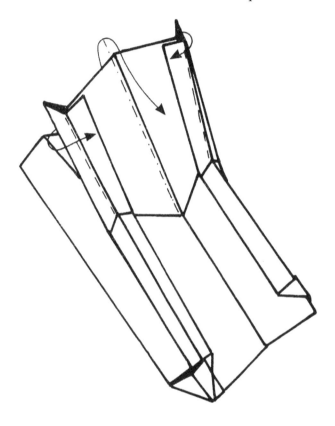

Flatten the fold with the new creases as shown in the step 6 image

Sailing Boat step 6

Fold the bow and stern corners as for the row boat.

Now you are ready to open out the boat sail and hull.

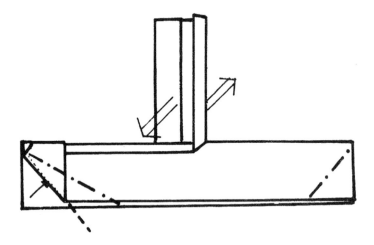

Open out the sail section by gently pulling apart the sides.

Crease the sail's side edges for reinforcement.

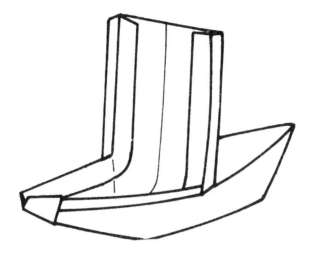

Your finished sailboat; take a deep breath and puff your lungs out to sail this across the bathtub!

Folding experiment...

Using a much longer piece of paper, it's possible to fold this craft so that it has two sails.

The beauty of this design is that it's made from one piece of paper with no separate add-ons requiring sticky tape or glue.

You'll need a length of paper that is around three times longer than the one you just folded.

I'll let you work out how!

Two-in-one Yacht

Although not shown in the image above, this is a yacht that has a jib which doubles as a small catamaran!

The jib can also be used as a keel to keep your yacht stable in rougher seas.

Two-in-one Yacht step 1

Make a square piece of paper out of A4 or Letter and then make a rabbit ear fold on one side of the diagonal crease. The Rabbit Ear fold is best described on page 12.

Please keep the cut-off section for the separate catamaran.

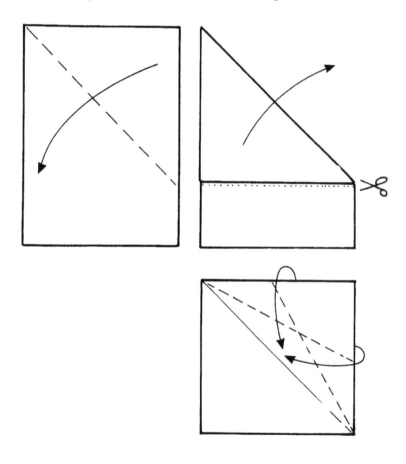

Two-in-one Yacht step 2

Make a mountain fold in half along the diagonal, except for the small rabbit ear triangle section.

In the lower image crease-fold well the bottom half of the hull. This will be pushed inwards in step 3.

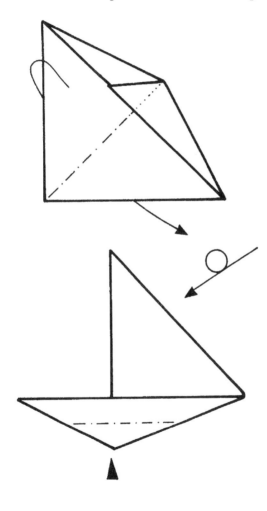

Two-in-one yacht step 3

Where you crease-folded the hull, hold model upside down, open out the fold and push in the center point to 'sink' it inside.

You should now have an aft-sail boat as shown in the lower image. Put this aside while we start the catamaran section.

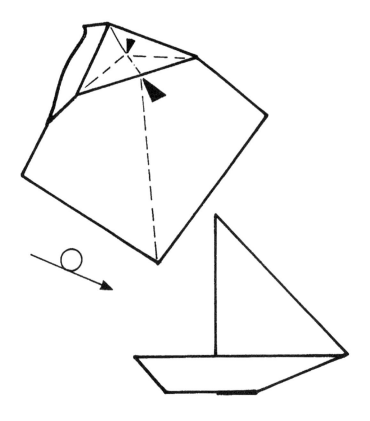

Two-in-one yacht step 4 – Catamaran section

Find the cut-off piece of paper you made earlier and make what is called a 'water bomb base' as follows:

Left image: make diagonal folds, and one horizontal fold behind.

Middle image: bring the sides together and fold down the top.

Right image: have it flattened as shown. Now fold bottom end up.

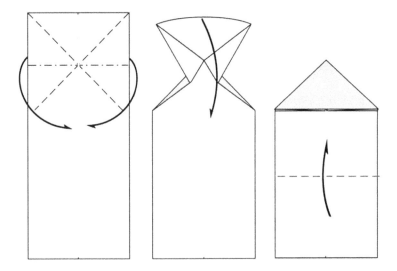

Two-in-one Yacht step 5 – Catamaran section

Left image: fold point down and up again on both sides. Crease well.

Right image: push in the middle section, similar to what you did in step 3, and bring in the sides again and flatten.

Lower image: it should look like this (upper part of model shown – larger view)

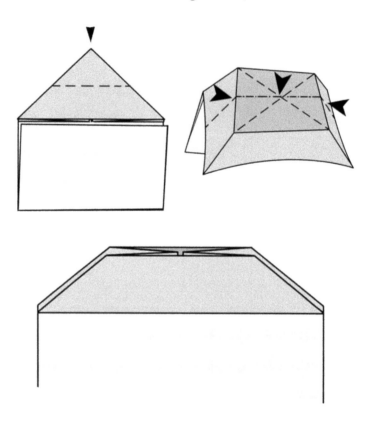

Two-in-one Yacht step 6 – Catamaran section

Have the model facing you as shown and fold flap 'C' behind to meet 'B', leaving the upper fold intact.

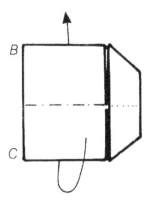

Two-in-one Yacht step 7 – Catamaran section

Fold corners 'C' and 'B' in to shape the sail and swing about to have your little Catamaran ready sailing.

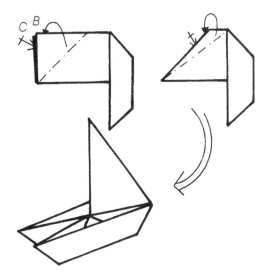

Two-in-one Yacht step 8 – Options

Your craft is nearly done. This image shows the options.

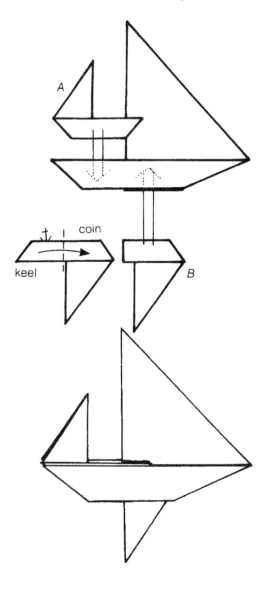

From the preceding image:

Top image: to add a jib on your main sailboat, slot the catamaran section into the larger sail boat's bow and hold in place with a small piece of tape.

Middle image: Alternatively, make a keel by folding the catamaran bow to the right (note orientation 'B' shown), adding a coin for ballast and slipping up *under* and *inside* the main sailboat's hull. Secure with tape.

Lower image in preceding page: do both keel and jib for a complete sailboat! Curve open the hull a little to ensure it will float.

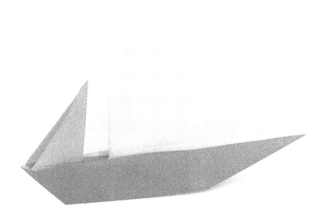

Yacht with jib

Easy Catamaran

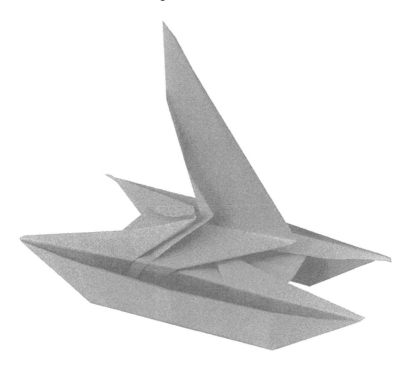

This is a very simple craft that moves well with good breezes.

This model uses a separate piece of paper for the sail section; it simply slots into place without the need for sticky tape.

Try experimenting with the sail section to improve the capture of breezes.

Try your own sail designs and race with your friends.

Easy Catamaran step 1

Make a square by first folding a diagonal and then cutting off the piece of paper which will be used later for the sail.

Lower image: make an opposite diagonal fold on the square and then fold the sides in to meet the center crease.

Don't forget to keep the cut-off piece - we'll need it for the sail!

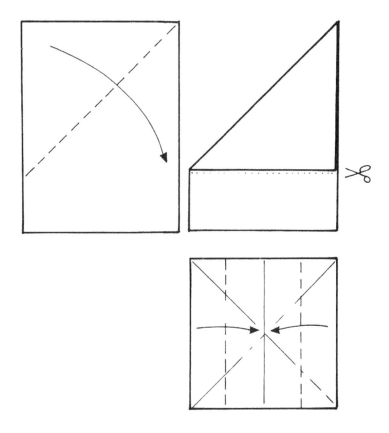

Easy Catamaran step 2

Left image: fold the paper behind in half.

Right image (larger view): fold the lower edges up in the approximate area shown.

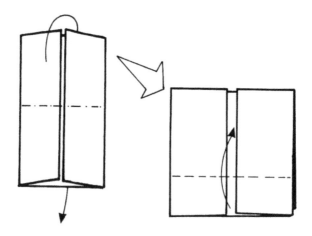

Easy Catamaran step 3

Pull out the sides, forming the hull section, and then repeat for the other side.

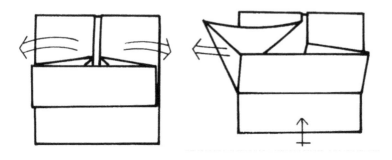

Easy Catamaran step 4

Crease-fold where shown to make the middle deck and open the sides, separating to make two hulls.

Lower image shows the model upside down; crease along the length of the inner hulls and then turn over.

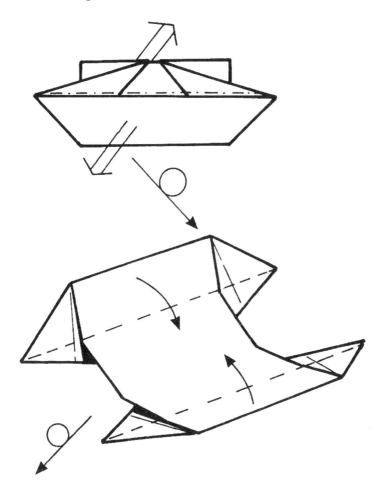

Easy catamaran step 5

The catamaran hull and middle deck is now ready to accept a sail which slots into the flap on the catamaran deck.

Steps for the sale are given on the following pages.

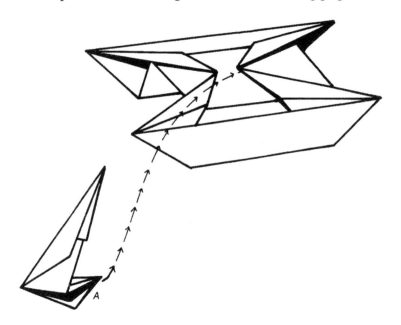

Easy Catamaran step 6 – sail section

Use the cut-off piece of paper (when you made the square).

For the upper two images, fold corners, and then rotate so it faces you as indicated for the right-hand image.

In the right-hand image, fold the point down diagonally to the left.

The bottom image is the result; fold this to the right.

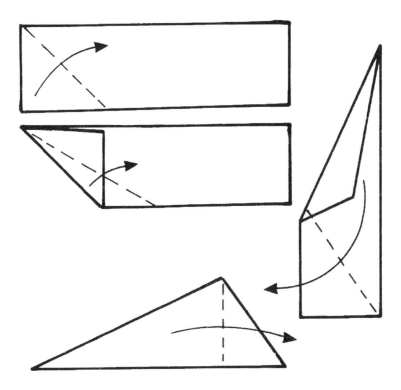

Easy Catamaran step 7 – sail section

Upper image: crease and then push in at the angle shown.

Middle image: swing up the sail to a vertical position. The pushed-in section acts as rigidity to keep the sail upright as shown in the lower right image.

Lower right image: 'A' is the flap that you slot snugly into the catamaran deck.

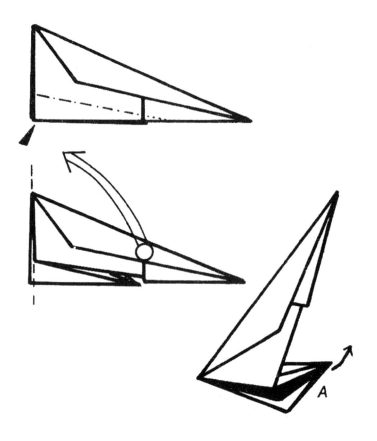

Easy Catamaran step 8

Insert the mainsail: slot the small triangle section 'A' into the upper deck section on the catamaran.

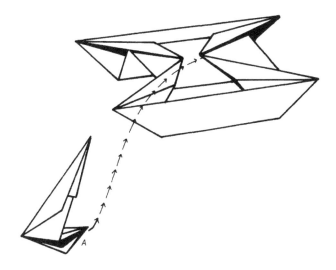

Now we're ready for cat racing!

Rich Dude Cruiser

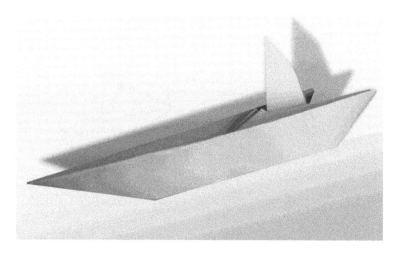

There are a few classy, expensive cruisers moored down at the marina near my place.

I once thought about buying a cheap 'doer-upper' that was for sale there but the amount of work involved would have taken me years to complete!

At least one can feel like the rich kid on the pontoon with one of these to grace the waters and the best thing is: no mooring costs!

Rich Dude Cruiser Step 1

Begin with a square folded and unfolded diagonally in half, and then fold the sides in to meet the center crease.

Right-hand image: tuck the small corners underneath and then fold in half.

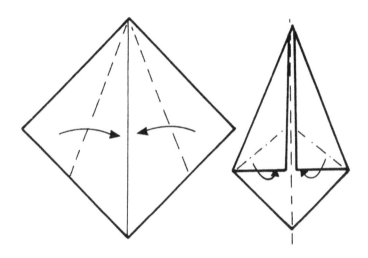

Rich Dude Cruiser step 2

With the model facing you as shown, crease-well and inverse fold inside and upwards, along the hidden flap edges that are inside.

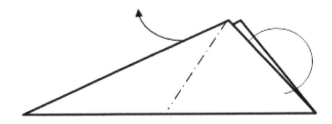

Rich Dude Cruiser step 3

Crease-fold the hull and then push in the bottom point of the boat's hull.

The lower image shows the boat upside-down and how the pushed-in folds are to be made. Collapse and flatten the new fold.

You should be used to this method by now :)

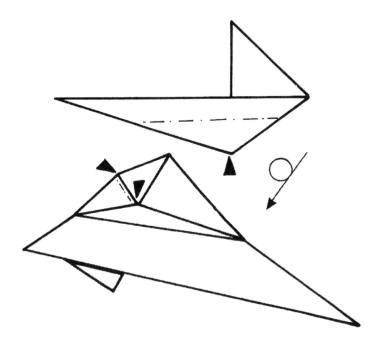

Rich Dude Cruiser step 4

Upper image: invert the 'sail' section; crease and swing it inside and down through the middle of the open-ended hull section.

Lower image: open out the stern section by swinging the downward-pointing triangle to the left.

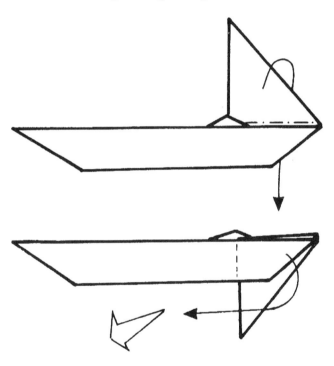

Rich Dude Cruiser step 5

Upper image shows a close-up of the triangle part of the open section.

Lower image: fold up the flap in the approximate position shown.

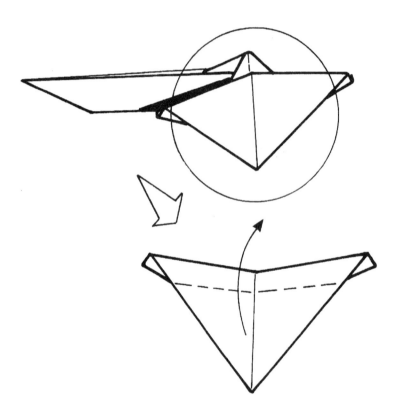

Rich Dude Cruiser step 6

Upper image: place thumb behind area 'A' and pull to the left, folding the flap towards the center. As you fold, the bottom right-hand corner showing the push-in symbol is automatically folded up and to the left also.

Lower image shows the fold done. Repeat for the left side and then fold 'B' and 'C' back together.

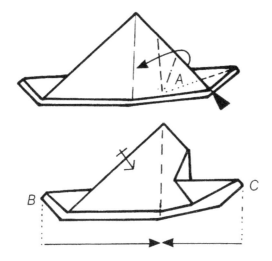

Your rich dude cruiser is now ready to show off.

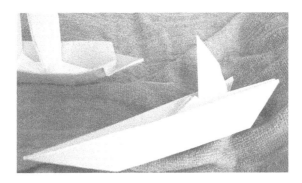

Seaplane

If folded using wax paper or other waterproof material, this plane will fly well and glide to a soft water landing, and float thereafter!

An actual demo of the craft landing on water is available on the YouTube channel *Paper Plane Lab*.

Seaplane step 1

Using Letter or A4 paper, make two diagonal creases and a horizontal one folded *behind* where the diagonals intersect; and in the bottom right image push the center in and then collapse the sides together.

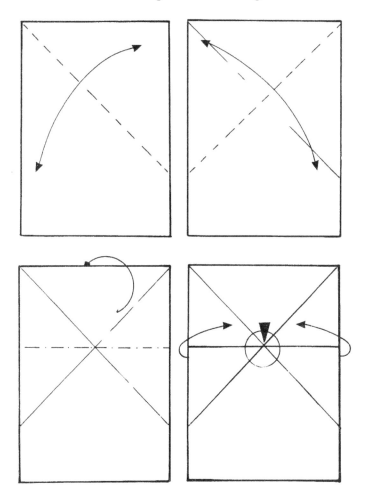

Seaplane step 2

The fold is near-complete; bring all the sides together and flatten the fold.

In the lower image (larger view), crease-fold in the approximate location indicated on both upper flaps. This will form the undercarriage.

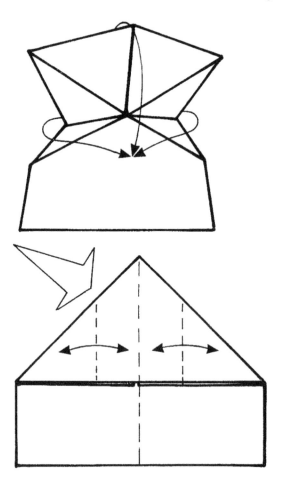

Seaplane step 3

Crease-fold the two corner points and then reverse-fold by placing your finger inside the corners and turning the points inside out, folding back over the edges above.

Lower image: you will need to open out the fold somewhat to make the reverse fold.

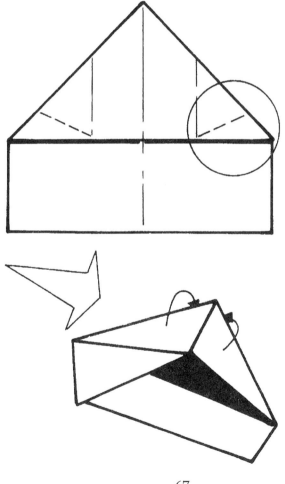

Seaplane step 4

Fold the nose back and then fold in half behind, down the length of the fuselage.

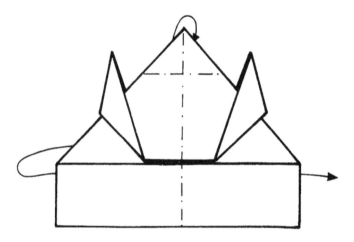

Seaplane step 5

Fold all the trailing edges; tail lift and side fins and then push in the lower right corner, all of which will serve to stop water getting over the wings.

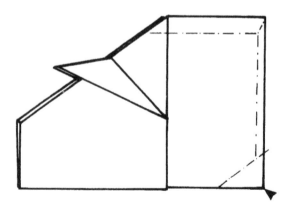

Seaplane step 6

Upper image: fold landing skis down, and then the wings.

Lower image: secure the wing-edge folds made in Step 5 by pushing in the corners and folding the points so they angle snug to the corner. Use tape to secure them if you wish. Some polymers, such as Mylar, are stiff enough not to need tape.

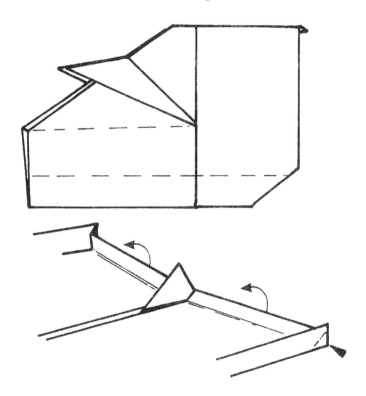

The completed seaplane; open out the water skis with your fingers so that they 'bow' out. This will help your craft stay afloat.

Spray with lacquer or vinyl spray paint for waterproofing and you're ready to fly and land on water.

Pirate Ship

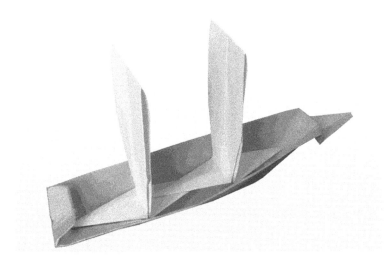

Ahoy there me 'earties; you scurvy lot will have to walk the plank if you can't make this fine vessel!

Well that's what Captain Flint says, but if you are like John Silver, you should be able to talk your way out of it!

Pirate Ship step 1

Fold a regular sheet of copy paper in half lengthwise and then fold the corners on each side of the flap that's facing you.

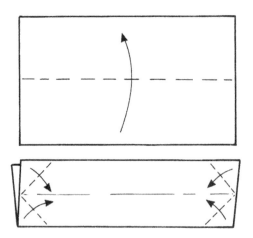

Pirate Ship step 2

Upper image: fold corners in again and turn over, and (lower image, larger view): fold corners on this side too.

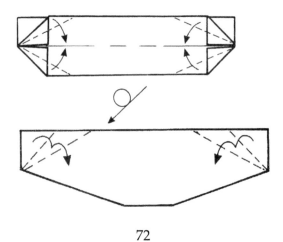

Pirate Ship step 3

Fold upper flap down and then crease-fold the bottom of the boat and push in, turning the model to view from the underside, shown in step 4.

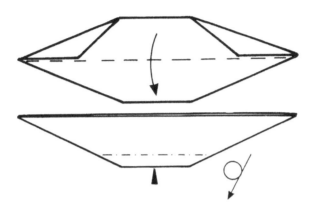

Pirate Ship step 4

Flatten the bottom, turn model around and then (lower image) reverse-fold the left section bow, and inverse-fold the right section stern.

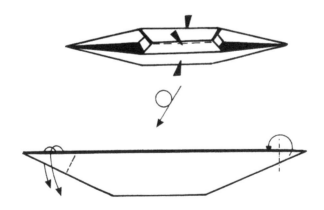

Pirate Ship step 5

Upper image: fold back the bow to make a nice pointed prow and fold in the stern.

Open the model out to look something like that shown in the lower image.

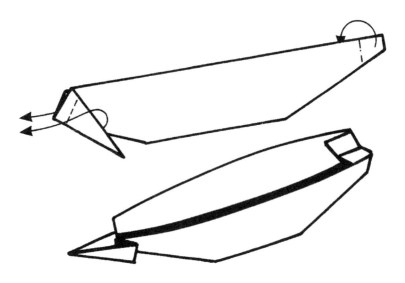

Pirate Ship step 6 – sail section

Let's now make some fine sails for our ship.

Cut another sheet of A4 or Letter paper lengthwise in half and then cut a half piece into two quarter strips for our two sails.

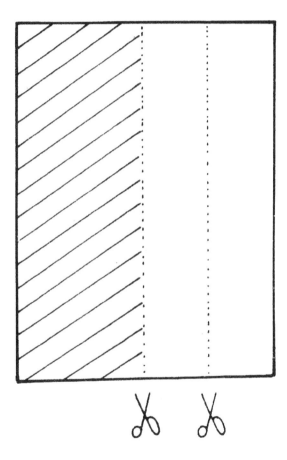

Pirate ship step 7 – sail section

Upper image: for each sail piece, crease-fold in half vertically and horizontally and then fold in the corners.

Center image: fold corners in again so that they overlap.

Lower image: fold across in half.

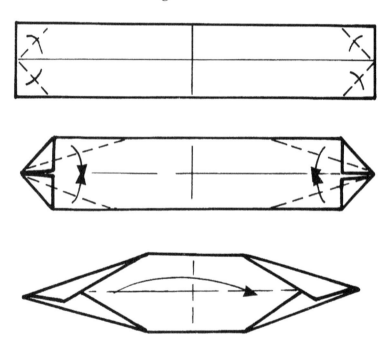

Pirate ship step 8 – sail section

Fold up the points on each side to be at right-angles to the sail to support mounting on the hull section.

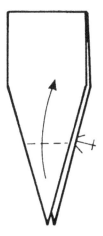

Pirate ship step 9 – sail section

Join the two sail sections together with tape.

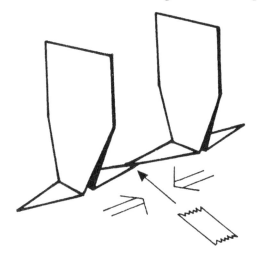

Pirate ship step 10 – sail section

Use tape to secure both sails to the boat.

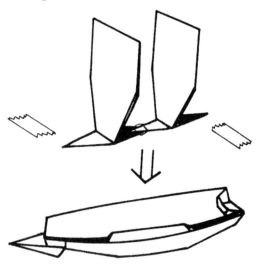

Paint skull and crossbones and you are now ready to sail the high seas, attack other vessels, rob them of their gold doubloons, force their crew to walk the plank, and all while talking like a pirate -arrgh!

Ocean Liner

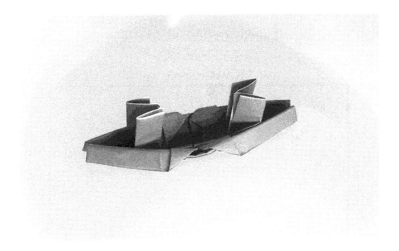

All that talk of pirating and looting may scare you from taking an ocean cruise, but this ship could be tempting.

The one shown here is small and floating in a bowl.

It's best to build a large one; use a larger piece of paper if you can, such as A3 or a bigger sheet of wax card.

Ocean liner step 1

Cut a sheet of paper in half lengthwise, crease fold the half-piece in half again and then fold edges in to meet the center crease.

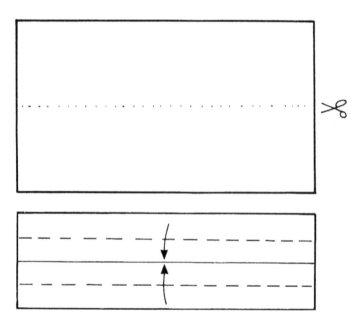

Ocean liner step 2

Fold ends in at one-third intervals, first the left end, and then the right.

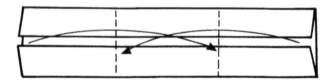

Ocean liner step 3

Fold upper left flap across to the right and then the edge underneath from the right to the left.

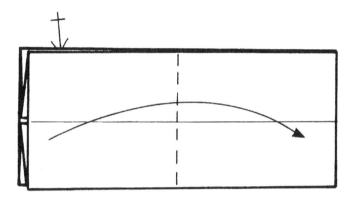

Ocean liner step 4

Fold the upper flaps, outer edges in, squashing the corners flat.

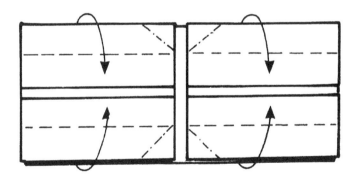

Ocean liner step 5

Fold lengthwise in half.

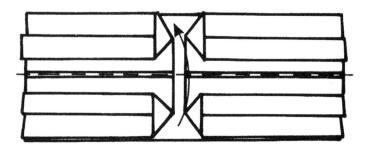

Ocean liner step 6

Lift the inside fold on the left and inverse fold to make the left smoke-stack. The lower image shows the fold nearly done. Repeat for the right stack and then flatten the fold.

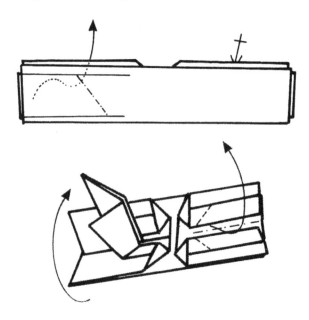

Ocean liner step 7

Smoke stacks done. Fold bow and stern corners in to complete the hull and then fold the horizontal edge down to make the railing, and repeat the railing fold on the other side.

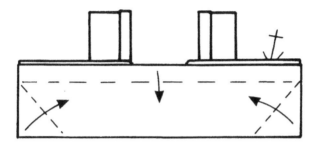

With fingers and thumb gently pull open the boat hull to give it a bowed shape. If the boat tips to one side, crease-fold near the bottom of the hull and push in the section as you did for some of the other boats in this book. This model works best when folded with large paper.

Your completed ocean liner; build a big one for your pool.

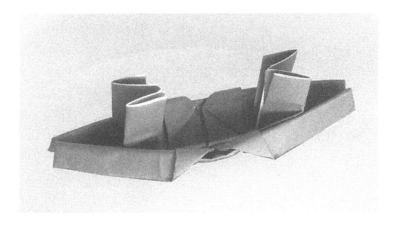

Ballast issues?

Depending on how well you made this craft, you may require some ballast to keep her upright.

Weight at the base of the hull is recommended, such as a paper clip or coin. If you make a larger vessel, try sticking a pen along the base of the hull for horizontal ballast.

Our little ship in the bowl floats well without any added ballast.

Aircraft Carrier

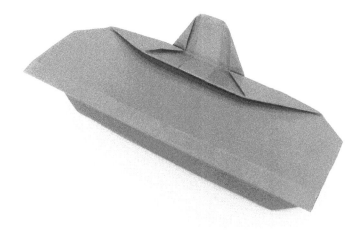

This is a tricky project in that you need to fold it correctly in order to have it float.

Once mastered, you can have a lot of fun trying to land your paper airplanes on a big aircraft carrier in your swimming pool.

If you do have ballast issues, there is a way to improve it without adding any extra weight, shown at the end of these instructions.

Aircraft Carrier step 1

Use a really big piece of paper or card. Cut the long edge off so you get a long rectangle. Now fold in half.

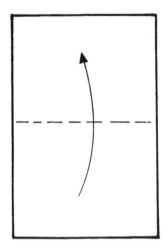

Aircraft Carrier step 2

Measure and inch and a half (approx. 4cm) from the bottom folded edge, crease fold and inverse the corners diagonally, and then fold down the flaps along the crease.

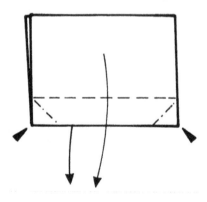

Aircraft Carrier step 3

Swing the flap that is behind back up and then fold its corners in diagonally.

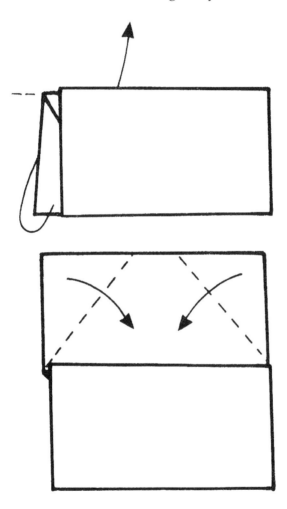

Aircraft Carrier step 4

Still on the same flap, fold top point down and then back up along the dashes. This flap will become the flight deck's 'control tower'.

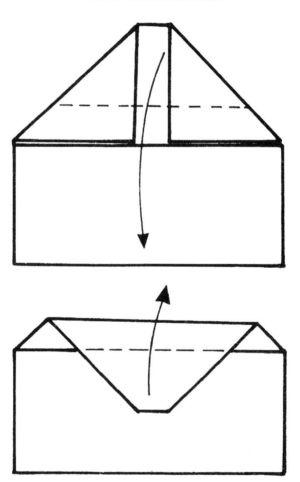

Aircraft Carrier step 5

Tuck fingers behind the flaps, pull towards the center and flatten.

Lower image: crease-fold along *xx* and *yy* and tuck under the flight control tower's long edge.

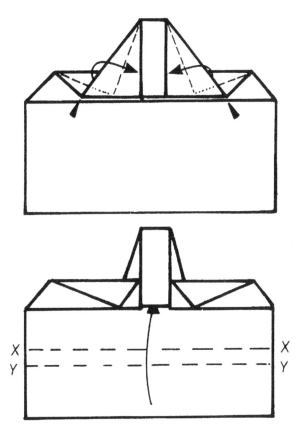

Aircraft Carrier step 6

Upper image: fold up the control tower section.

Lower image: open the hull to create a new fold as shown in *xx*. This will create a wider hull in which to create ballast (which can be a heavy pen, drill bit, line of coins etc.).

Tape the flight control tower section to the flight deck to secure the fold. Fold corners A and B behind to secure the hull.

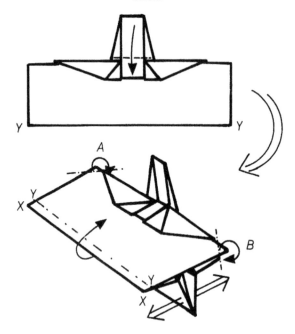

Your aircraft carrier should float, however If you want a floating craft without needing added ballast weight, try the following steps…

Aircraft Carrier step 7 – hull modification

Turn your model upside down and crease-fold well the bottom of the hull section. We will push this section in as we have done for other boats in this book. Crease well.

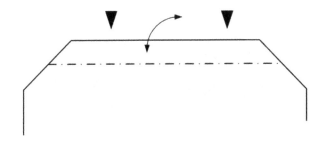

Aircraft Carrier step 8 – hull modification

With the model upside down, open out your model and push inwards along the bottom of the hull.

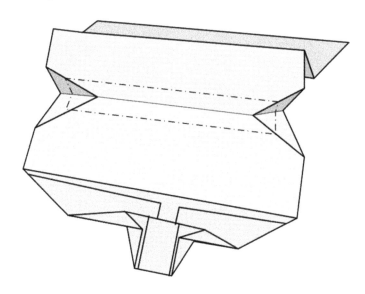

Aircraft Carrier step 9 – hull modification

Collapse in the pushed-in fold on each end and it will look like the left image. Push in the corners to reinforce the hull.

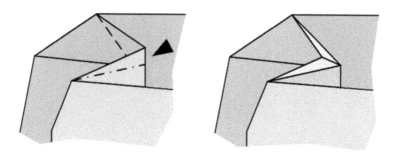

Here is a close-up photo of the modified underside.

And you are done!

Bring the ship together again, noting step 6.

Your completed aircraft carrier; if you want to use even larger sheets of paper or card (or waterproof card), ensure the folds are well-creased.

Use spray lacquer to help waterproof your craft, and for a fun competition, try and land your paper airplanes on it.

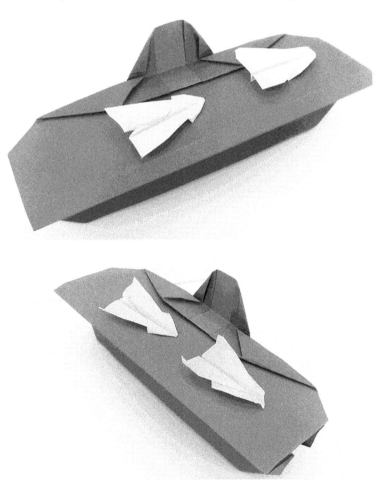

Milton Keynes UK
Ingram Content Group UK Ltd.
UKHW050052180624
444226UK00014B/542